# REUNION

---

# DARK PONY

*Other Plays by David Mamet*
*Published by Grove Press*


*American Buffalo*

*A Life in the Theatre*

*Sexual Perversity in Chicago* and *The Duck Variations*

*The Water Engine* and *Mr. Happiness*

*The Woods*

# *REUNION*

## *DARK PONY*

Two Plays by

# DAVID MAMET

Grove Press, Inc.
New York

First Evergreen Edition 1979
First Printing 1979
ISBN: 0–394–17459–3
Grove Press ISBN: 0–8021–4258–3
Library of Congress Catalog Card Number: 79–2319

Library of Congress Cataloging in Publication Data

Mamet, David.
Reunion; Dark Pony.

I. Mamet, David. Dark Pony. 1979. II. Title: Reunion.
PS3563.A4345R4    812'.5'4    79–2319
ISBN 0–394–17459–3 pbk.

Manufactured in the United States of America

Distributed by Random House, Inc., New York

GROVE PRESS, INC., 196 West Houston Street,
New York, N.Y. 10014

# REUNION

*Reunion* was first produced by the St. Nicholas Theater Company, Chicago, Illinois, on January 9, 1976, with the following cast:

BERNIE CARY                    Don Marston

CAROL MINDLER                  Linda Kimbrough

This production was directed by Cecil O'Neal.

The Yale Repertory production of *Reunion* opened in New Haven, Connecticut, on October 14, 1977, with the following cast:

BERNIE CARY                    Michael Higgins

CAROL MINDLER                  Lindsay Crouse

This production was directed by Walt Jones; set by Kate Edmunds; lighting by William Connor.

## The Characters

CAROL MINDLER, twenty-four years old
BERNIE CARY, her father

## The Scene

Bernie's apartment.

## The Time

Sunday afternoon in early March.

# *Scene I*

BERNIE: I would of recognized you anywhere.
>It is you. Isn't it?
>Carol. Is that you?
>You haven't changed a bit.
>I would of recognized you anywhere. . . .
>This is a very important moment.
>But there's no reason why we should have it in the hall so let me take your coat. . . .
>I feel like a racehorse. You ever go to the track?
>Well, that's what I feel like.
>If I was still drinking, I'd offer you a drink.
>If I was still drinking, you probably wouldn't be here.
>That's all right.

CAROL: Bernie . . .

BERNIE: You're not going to call me Dad, or like that? . . .
>Thank God.
>So here we are.

CAROL: Yes.

BERNIE: So how you been?

CAROL: Fine.

BERNIE: Great.

CAROL: You?

BERNIE: Since the last time you saw me, mainly bad, lately good. You look wonderful.

CAROL: You don't look so bad yourself. For an old man. You take good care of yourself.

BERNIE: Well, I better. Who else is going to take care of me? . . .
The VA, of course. They take pretty good care of me, I'm forced to admit.
I still go to see them about three times a year for my back.
They take good care of you in the hospital.
The guys at A.A., I don't see them much anymore.
Thank God. They took pretty good care of me.
I hated those sonofabitches. . . .
Frank over at the place. He took care of me for a while.
Five there, ten here . . . he gave me a job.
Knows the restaurant business like the back of his hand.
I've been a very lucky guy.

CAROL: You've got a lot of friends, Bernie.

BERNIE: Always have.
For some reason.
You take pretty good care of yourself.

CAROL: Got to.

BERNIE: Yeah.

CAROL: The A.A. are the ones who put us in touch with you.

Gerry went.
He said they seemed like very nice people.

BERNIE: Very contrite.
You still go to church?

CAROL: No. Nobody goes to church anymore. *(Pause.)*
You still go to church?

BERNIE: I never went to church. Since I was a kid.
Easter.

CAROL: We should both go.
Renew our faith.
Gerry goes to church.

BERNIE: Yeah? Does he mean it?

CAROL: Who knows.

BERNIE: He might mean it. You never know. . . .
Some of 'em mean it.

# Scene II

BERNIE: Goddamn, it's good to see you.
It's good to see you.

CAROL: This apartment is very nice.

BERNIE: I did it myself. Leslie, my friend, she helped.
Quite a lot, actually . . . to put the place in the state
it's in now.
But the basic place . . . I furnished it.
Fixed it up.
Been here two years plus. . . .
I'm glad you like it.


CAROL: Our place is quite nice. You'll like it a lot.
When you come see it. You have to come out. Very
soon.
I did it myself.
It's so comfortable.
It's a real home, you know?
It's just five rooms.
It gets a little cramped when the kids are there.
Gerry's kids.
They sleep in the living room. . . .
They're good kids.
Gerry has a study.
We're very comfortable there.


BERNIE: You got a doorman?


CAROL: Yes. . . .
The building's very safe.
Lots of light and air.
We're thinking of building a house. *(Pause.)*
This place really is lovely, Bernie.


BERNIE: What can I tell you.

## *Scene III*

CAROL *(sees bomber group picture)*: Are you in there?

BERNIE: Yeah.

CAROL: I'm going to pick you out.

BERNIE: That's a long time ago.

CAROL *(indicates)*: There!

BERNIE: That's me.
　　I haven't changed, huh?

CAROL: Bernie Cary. Army Air Corps.

BERNIE: Butch. They called me Butch then.

CAROL: Why?

BERNIE: . . . I couldn't tell you to save my life.
　　Those were strange times.

CAROL: What's this?

BERNIE: It's a medal.
　　Sit down. Sit down. It's nothing.
　　I fought. I did my bit.
　　If you want to know about your father
　　I was a tail gunner.

I shot a machine gun. Big deal.
They had a life expectancy of—you know what?—
Three missions. Three.
What the hell. You can get killed in a steel mill,
right?
But I'm no hero.
They put you in a plane with a gun, it pays to shoot
at the guys who are trying to kill you.
Where's the courage in that. . . .
But you didn't have to take anything.
From nobody.
That was all right.
Anybody get wise—some wiseass Lieutenant—
I say:
"Shove it, Champ. I'm a fuckin' tail gunner
on a B-17,
and I don't take no shit from some chicken
Lieutenant."
And I didn't. From Anybody.
So what does that make me.
You would like England.

CAROL: I've been there.

BERNIE: You've been there? What? With your new husband?

CAROL: With him and by myself.

BERNIE: Where else you been?

CAROL: Jamaica. Around the States.

BERNIE: See America First, huh?
I worked a year in San Francisco. In a body shop.

CAROL: I've been in San Francisco.

BERNIE: Some fine people in San Francisco.

CAROL: Oh, yes.

BERNIE: And a lot of assholes.

CAROL: Lot of assholes all over.

BERNIE: Aah, people are people, you know?
Tell me about your new husband.

CAROL: I want to know about you.

BERNIE: And I want to know about you.
So. Does he love you?
I swear I'll kill the sonofabitch, so tell me the truth.

CAROL: He loves me.

BERNIE: And you love him?

CAROL: Yes.

BERNIE: So where's the story in that?

CAROL: No story.
Just the usual.

BERNIE: So it's not "the usual" for nothing.
These things work out. They work themselves out.
Is he a good guy?

CAROL: He's. . . .
He's a good guy. I think he's frightened of women.

BERNIE: He's frightened of you? . . .
That's funny.
But you know, never having been a man, you
don't know—
but a lot of men are frightened of women,
let me tell you.

Beautiful women especially can be frightening.
There's no shame in that.
He takes good care of you.

CAROL: Yes.

BERNIE: So what do you want?

CAROL: I want to hear about you.

BERNIE: What's to tell? You see it all here. Have a look.
Fifty-three years old.
Ex-alcoholic.
Ex-this.
Ex-that.
Democrat.
You smoke pot?

CAROL: No. You?

BERNIE: Nope.
Tried it once. Don't like the taste.
When I was a drunk I never drank anything but the best.
Saw no reason to change my style of life simply because I happened to be an alcoholic.
Taste. . . .
Never bummed for change. Waste of time.
Bill. Two bills, bounce a check.
Respectable.
If you're a drunk, you'd better be respectable. . . .
1951 I lost my license. Fourteen citations for drunk driving in the month of December 1951.
You were what? Four.
I was living on the Cape.
You and your mother were in Newton.

CAROL: What were you doing?

BERNIE: In 1951 I was in the Vet's Hospital awhile with
my back.
The rest of the time I was working for the Phone
Company.
Worked for the Phone Company ten years.
I was seeing this girl in Boston.
Your mother and I were split . . .
I got that court order in 1951.
You know . . .
Did you know I wanted to see you?
Did they tell you anything?
I wanted to come see you, you know.
I couldn't see you because of that court order.

CAROL: I don't know. They told me . . . something.

BERNIE *(Pause)*: I was a mover for a year.
Cross country.
I missed my brother's funeral. Your Uncle Alex.
You never met him. Did you ever meet Alex?

CAROL: Yes.

BERNIE: He's dead now. 1962.
And his wife, Lorraine, won't talk to me since I
missed his funeral.
I'm sorry I missed it, too. But what the hell.
Life goes on. And when he died I was out west
someplace with American Van Lines and I didn't
even know about it 'til September. . . .
You wanna hear a story?

CAROL: Sure do.

BERNIE: I'll tell you a story. So I'd been drunk at the time for several years and was walking down Tremont Street one evening around nine and here's this big van in front of a warehouse and the driver is ringing the bell in the shipping dock trying to get in (which he won't do, because they moved a couple of weeks ago and the warehouse is deserted. But he doesn't know that.)

So I say, "Hey, you looking for Hub City Transport?" And he says yeah, and I tell him they're over in Lechmere. So he says "Where?" So I tell him I don't know the address but I can take him there. Which was, of course, a bunch of shit, but I figured maybe I could make a couple of bucks on the deal. And why not.

So I ride over to Lechmere.

I find the warehouse.

You ever been to Lechmere?

CAROL: Just passing through.

BERNIE: Very depressing.

So, anyway. He's in Lechmere to pick up a load.

And he offers me ten bucks to help him load the van.

So fine. Later we go across the street for a cup of coffee and he gives me this story. He just fired his partner, he likes the way I handle furniture, and do I want a job?

Hey, what the hell.

We finish the coffee and off we go.

And for one year I didn't get home, never shaved, wore the same goddamn clothes, slept in the cab, made some money, spent some money, saw the country. Alex died, and I missed his funeral.

Which, of course, is why Lorraine won't talk to me.
Because I got back in September and I'm back a
day or so and I go over to Alex's.
Lorraine answers the door and I tell her,
"Lorraine, tell your fat-ass husband to grab his coat
because we are going to the track." He loved the
track.
And she says: "If I ever catch you in my sight again,
drunk or sober, I'm going to punch your fucking
heart out."
Which were harsh words for her.
And to this day—she believed I was in town and
drunk at the time of the funeral—not once have I
seen or spoken to her in ten years. . . .
And we were very close at one time.
She was a good woman.
Very loyal. . . .
Alex fought in the war.
What the hell. How's your mother?

CAROL: Good.

BERNIE: What about the guy she married?

CAROL: Good.
You know, he's a hell of a man.

BERNIE: No! Don't doubt it for a second.
I never met the sonofabitch, but I'd stake my life
on it. . . .
You got any kids?

CAROL: No.

BERNIE: Didn't think so. How long you been married?

CAROL: Two years. Gerry's got two kids.

BERNIE: You told me. How old?

CAROL: Twelve and eight. Boys.

BERNIE: How are they?

CAROL: They're good boys.

BERNIE: You like 'em?

CAROL: We get along.

BERNIE: They like you?

CAROL: You know how it is.

BERNIE: Their other mother died?

CAROL: Divorced.

BERNIE: . . . I like him, Gerry. He seems like an all right guy.
A thoughtful guy. . . .
Jesus, he gave me a moment, though.
I come into the restaurant and Frank—Frank's the owner—he says, "Bernie, there's a guy outside askin for Butch Cary."
Now, I haven't called myself Butch since I'm on the wagon, three years.
I was called Butch from the days in the Air Corps, and all my old drunk partners know me as Butch.
So. I figure it's some old acquaintance looking for a handout, or a bill collector. Because he called me Butch.
So I peek out the kitchen door and there's this real nice-looking guy around forty—what am I telling you what he looks like—
Anyway, it's obvious he's not a bill collector, and

he's not looking for a handout, and I don't know
him from Adam.
So I get out of the kitchen—he probably told you
this stuff—
I still got my coat on 'cause I just walked in the back
door . . .
I guess I looked kind of suspicious—who
wouldn't—and I go over to him and he says,
"Are you Butch Cary?"
And I say, "Yeah, who are you?"
He says, "I'm Gerry Mindler. I'm Carol's husband.
Your daughter."
I told him I know who my daughter is.
I told him, "Mister, I am one tough sonofabitch, but
I'll be goddamned if I don't feel like I'm gonna bust
out crying."
And I almost did.

# Scene IV

BERNIE: You got a brother you never met, you know,
  a half-brother. Marty.
  My and Ruth's kid. Ruth, my second wife. You
  could call her your stepmother . . . if it made any
  sense.
  I know your mother had another daughter.

CAROL: Barbara.

BERNIE: I know.

CAROL: We're very close.

BERNIE: I don't doubt it.

CAROL: We are.

BERNIE: Marty. You'd like him.

CAROL: How is he?

BERNIE: I haven't seen him now in several years. He's say three years younger than you. He's a good kid.

CAROL: What does he do?

BERNIE: Do?
The last time I heard—and this might of changed —nothing.

CAROL: What was Ruth like?

BERNIE: Like your mother, I'm sorry to say.
Not that she wasn't a lovely woman.
And not that your . . .

CAROL: . . . It's okay.

BERNIE: Anyway, we didn't get along too long. And your mother was not such a hotshot either, to get down to it.
Ruth never understood me. I take it back, she understood me. When Marty was young. We got along.

CAROL: And then?

BERNIE: I left her. These things happen.

But, Jesus, he was a fine little kid.

Having kids, Carol, is something no one can describe.

Having your own kids is . . . indescribable.

I mean it.

You were quite a little kid.

We used to have a good time.

Going to the zoo . . .

Do you remember that? Do you remember what you used to say when I came home?

Three years old?

I'd come in the door.

You'd say: "Hi there, Pop!"

I don't know where you picked that up. I guess your mother used to coach you.

Do you remember that?

Do you remember going to the Science Museum? We used to be over there every week. See the locomotive . . .

The steam engines, you remember that?

You were a beautiful kid.

You were everything to your mother and me.

I still got the pictures.

You want to see how cute you were? You wait here. Just sit there.

You know who took those? Alex took those at his house . . .

Fourth of July 1950. It was the first year he had his new house.

You probably don't remember.

Took them with his Brownie.

You were crying for some reason, and I said, "Look

at the camera, baby. . . ." I'll be goddamned if I
know where those pictures are.

CAROL: It's okay.

BERNIE: They're around here somewhere.

CAROL: It's okay, Bernie.

BERNIE: But where can they be?
I look at 'em constantly. . . .
You want some coffee?

CAROL: No, thanks.

BERNIE: You smoke too much.

CAROL: I know it.

BERNIE: Your husband smoke?

CAROL: Yes.

BERNIE: Does he tell you to cut down?

CAROL: Yes.

BERNIE: They're no good for you.

CAROL: I know.

BERNIE: He should set an example.

CAROL: He's my husband, Bernie, not my father.

BERNIE: I don't smoke.
I gave it up.
When I went on the wagon.
Did I tell you I'm thinking about getting married
again?

CAROL: No.

BERNIE: It's not definite. Not yet.
I'm just thinking.
Leslie. She works at the restaurant. Gerry met her.

CAROL: Tell me about her.

BERNIE: . . . She knows me. I know her.
I respect her.
She's a good worker, she knows my past.
I think she loves me. She's about forty. . . .
Was married once.
It's like a habit.
How would you, you know . . . feel if I got married again?
Would that . . . do anything to you?
I realize you don't have a long basis for comparison.

CAROL: I think it would be good for you.

BERNIE: You think that, huh?

CAROL: Yes.

BERNIE: Of course it wouldn't get in the way of our getting to know each other.

CAROL: Why are you getting married again?

BERNIE: . . . Companionship.

## Scene V

BERNIE: But I'm a happy man now. And I don't use the term loosely.

I got a good job at the restaurant.

I've stopped drinking. I'm putting a little money away.

CAROL: I'm glad to hear it.

BERNIE: Well, there's nothing wrong with it.

For the first time in a long time I get a kick out of what I'm doing.

I enjoy it at work. Everybody knows me. They respect me.

I spend a lot of time walking. Just walking in the Common.

After all this time. Not to cadge a drink. Or to get laid.

Excuse me. . . .

People always talk about going out to the country or getting back to nature and all the time I say, "Yeah, yeah," and what does it mean?

I see the logic of it, but it means nothing to me.

Because my entire life I'm looking for a way around.

Do you know what I mean?

Like drinking, certainly, or with your mother, or my second wife.... Being in debt—there was never a reason for all that money trouble—and changing jobs all the time . . . so what does it get me but dumber and dumber, and I'm a cynic.

But now . . .

On the other hand, it's about time—I mean, I'm fifty-three years old. I've spent the majority of my life drinking and, when you come right down to it, being a hateful sonofabitch. . . .

But you, married. Living well. You live well.

A nice guy. A fine guy for a husband.

Going to have . . . maybe . . . kids.

You shouldn't let it bother you, but you have a lot of possibilities. Don't you feel that?

CAROL: I do.

BERNIE: Well, then. The rest is not very important.

It's for the weaklings.

No, really. And I like people as much as the next guy.

It's for the sissies and the drinkers—which I was—who need it.

Otherwise . . . What have you got to lose?

Take a chance.

You got to take your chance for happiness.

You got to grab it.

You got to know it and you got to want it.

And you got to *take* it.

Because all the possessions in the world can't take it for you.

Do you know what I'm talking about? . . .

It's a fucking jungle out there. And you got to learn

the rules because *nobody's* going to learn them for you.

You wanna drink? Go drink.

You wanna do *this?* Pay the price.

Always the price. Whatever it is.

And you gotta know it and be prepared to pay it if you don't want it to pass you by.

And if you don't know that, you gotta find it out, and that's all I know.


# Scene VI


BERNIE: I don't care.

1950, 1970. *(Pause.)*

You know what I mean.

What's on my mind now is getting to know you.

And maybe getting married again.

You look good. Jesus, you are a good-looking young woman.

CAROL: I get it all from you.

BERNIE: Aaah . . .

CAROL: I used to think you were the handsomest man I ever saw.

You used to look just like Tonto.

BERNIE: Tonto?

CAROL: The Indian. The Lone Ranger's friend.

BERNIE: I know who Tonto is.

CAROL: It was my secret. I was sure you were Tonto.
I asked you once.
You remember?

BERNIE: No.

CAROL: You said, "No, of course not."
I was very upset. I didn't know why you were lying
to me.

BERNIE: I'm sorry.

CAROL: I was about four.
I never told anyone.
I thought that it was our secret. *(Pause.)*
You wanted me to keep our secret. *(Pause.)*

BERNIE: Thank you.

CAROL: Bernie . . .

BERNIE: What?

CAROL: Bernie, you're wasted in the restaurant. Do you
know that?

BERNIE: I like it at the restaurant.
I love it at the restaurant.
It's where I work. Leslie works there.
What do you mean?

CAROL: I mean . . .

BERNIE: I mean who do you think you're talking to?
This is not Tonto the Indian but Butch Cary, ex-
drunk.

The only two worthwhile things I ever did in my life were work for the Phone Company and fire a machine gun, and I can't do either of them anymore, not that I feel sorry for myself, but I'm just telling you.

I mean I am what I am and that's what happiness comes from . . . being just that. Don't you agree?

. . . I mean you must remember that your mother was a very different sort of person from me. As is, I'm sure, the guy she married. And the way you're brought up, though all very well and good . . . is not basically my life, as fine as it may be and I hope it brings you a lot of happiness.

I mean, you haven't even *been* to the restaurant, for chrissakes. . . .

It's very clean and . . .

CAROL: No, I'm sure it's . . . I only meant . . .

BERNIE: I know what you meant.

I know what you're talking about.

But lookit, my life needn't be your life in any sense of the word, you know?

I like it like I am, and if you find that the people you . . . go with, your friends and so on . . .

CAROL: Don't be silly, Bernie.

BERNIE: I'm not being silly.

CAROL: Yes, you are, and that's the last I want to say about it.

BERNIE: Okay, but . . .

CAROL: So for chrissakes, knock it off, okay?

## *Scene VII*

BERNIE: I gotta admit it. I knew you were coming over.
I was scared.

CAROL: Yes, me too.

BERNIE: There's nothing wrong in that.

CAROL: No.

BERNIE: After all, what were we going to expect . . .
Red Sails in the Sunset? . . .
What do you do now? I mean . . .

CAROL: I work for Gerry. At the Office.

BERNIE: You're a secretary?

CAROL: I'm just kind of . . . everything.

BERNIE: It sounds great.

CAROL: It actually has a lot of responsibility.

BERNIE: As long as you like it, right?

CAROL *(Pause)*: Right.

BERNIE: So quit. . . .
Anyway, it's not the end of the world.

CAROL:  No. *(Pause.)* No. *(Pause.)* We're not . . . sleeping together much anymore.

BERNIE:  Oh.

CAROL:  And that's only *part* of it.

BERNIE:  What's the rest of it?
*(Pause.)*
Come on, let me tell you something. You know what my advice to you is?
"Don't let it get you down."

CAROL:  He's not such a great lover, anyway.

BERNIE:  He seems like a nice enough guy.

CAROL:  He's a lousy fuck.

BERNIE:  That doesn't mean he isn't a nice guy, Carol.

CAROL:  What do you know about it?

BERNIE:  Speaking as your father and as a guy with quite an experience of the world . . .

CAROL:  . . . whatever . . .

BERNIE:  . . . not a hell of a lot. But I'll tell you, he's genuinely fond of you. . . .
That's got to count for something . . .
Right?

# *Scene VIII*

CAROL: You know—when I was young they used to talk
about Broken Homes.
Today, nothing. Everyone's divorced. Every kid on
the block's got three sets of parents.
But . . .
It's got to have affected my marriage. . . .
I came from a Broken Home.
The most important institution in America.

BERNIE: Life goes on. Your mother and me . . .

CAROL: . . . Oh, yeah, life goes on. And no matter how
much of an asshole you may be, or may have been,
life goes on.
Gerry's like that.

BERNIE: I'm not going to lie to you. I felt guilt and
remorse and every other goddamn thing. I missed
you.
What the hell.
I was mad. I was mad at your mother. I was mad at
you.
I was mad at the fucking government that never
treated me like anything but a little kid. . . . saving
their ass with daylight precision bombing. . . .

Everybody hates the VA.

I mean, understand: I'm not asking you to understand me, Carol, because we've both been through enough.

Am I right?

*Pause.*

CAROL: Gerry was in Korea.

BERNIE: Yes? And what does he have to say about it?

CAROL: Nothing.

# Scene IX

BERNIE: Let me tell you a story.

One time—this was strange—when I'm working for the Phone Company. I'm out on the Cape. Lineman.

Repairs, on the street. I'm making out okay, what with that and my disability.

Bought myself a new Buick.

Beautiful sonofabitch. Used to drive into Boston and go out to Wonderland with Alex.

He loved that car. I think he was secretly envious.

And so I'm working out on the Cape. It's December thirtieth.

I get invited to a New Year's party in Provincetown. I'm supposed to be working.

So I call in sick. What the hell, I had a good work record.

And it's New Year's Eve day and I'm getting ready to drive to Provincetown.

Put a hundred bucks in my wallet and I go to Mitchell's—that's the tavern in Falmouth I used to hang out at—and there's this Italian kid shooting pool. About twenty. I don't know . . . Steve, something like that.

So I offer him twenty bucks to drive out to Provincetown with me, stay in the car, and drive me home New Year's Day.

So fine. We get up to Provincetown, I go over to Kenny's house . . . Kenny Hill. You would of liked him I think. He would have liked you, I can tell you that. Had an eye for younger women. Who could blame him.

And so we had a hell of a party.

That's one thing Kenny knew how to do is throw a party.

But the point is not the party but the next morning. So the next morning I get up off the couch or wherever I was and put on my coat and go out to the car to invite this kid Steve in for a cup of coffee or something.

So there's the Buick but the kid is gone. Nowhere to be found. Vanished. Along with my flashlight, which I don't find out til I rack the car up near Truro. *(Pause.)* But hold on. *(He thinks for a moment.)*

I think he took my flashlight. . . . *(Pause.)*

So I go back in the house. Get myself together, and

I figure I'd better start back to Falmouth. I'm hung over as a sonofabitch. I say good-bye to my friends, grab a bottle, and into the car.

It's snowing up a storm. I can hardly see anyway. I'm weaving all over the road. Next thing I know I'm asleep. And the following thing I'm wrapped around a telephone pole.

So I get out. Knocked the pole clean over; the hood of the Buick is wrenched to shit. I go to get out the flashlight to try to get a look at the engine, and the flashlight's gone.

There's no help for it, so I get back in and go to sleep.

Next thing I know here comes a Black and White. The cop wakes me up, I happen to know him from around Falmouth, and I convince him that it's all an accident, and I give him a drink and he drives me home and promises to call the garage. So you should be careful who you're calling a pig.

Any case, I no sooner get in bed than ten seconds later, Wham! The telephone rings and it's Jim Daugherty, the supervisor for the Cape.

"How are you feeling?" he asks.

"Like a big piece of cow shit," I tell him.

"You gotta come in today," he says.

"Jim," I tell him, "I'm sick, it's New Year's, get someone else."

"Everybody else is drunk," he says. "I'm the only one here, and some asshole knocked down a pole near Truro."

. . . So I tell him my car won't start. He says he's coming over in the truck to get me.

So I make some coffee and he comes and we go over to Truro to fix the pole.

He's cursing the whole way:
"Jagoff" this and "Asshole" that . . .
And what with the overtime and holiday pay and
the twenty Jim slipped me for coming along I made
about ninety bucks for one afternoon. And Jim was
so mad, he did most of the work himself and I spent
most of the time in the cab drinking.

# Scene X

BERNIE:  But I can't work for the Phone Company any-
more.
When they finally pulled my license, that was it.
I hit a cop car. Actually it sounds more exciting
than it was. It was an unmarked car. He was parked
anyway. Only time I ever got a ticket in Boston. A
heartbreaker.
Anyway, I lost my license and that was it. I got fired
and they meant it.
Jim Daugherty went down to Boston to talk to 'em.
No Dice.
He even wrote a letter to the Board of Trustees for
me.
The Board of Trustees of the Phone Company.
No good.
He said if I got fired he was going to quit, too.
. . . He didn't, though. . . .

But he would've. . . .
Broke him up, too. Best goddamn lineman on the Cape.
Eight years, best record.
We were very close. . . .
Canned. Like that. Pension, benefits, seniority.
Shot. . . .
It was probably for the best.
But I'll be goddamned if I can see how.
I used to drink a bit on the job. But who didn't?
Jim knew that. Nobody cared.
If it hadn't showed up in the accident report, I'd be working today.
What the hell.

CAROL: How long till you can get your license back?

BERNIE: Supposedly never, but, actually, in about a year.
They review it.
They told me about it at the A.A. The guys there go up with you.
Their opinion is very respected.

CAROL: I was a teacher for a while.

BERNIE: You were? Where?

CAROL: In Newton. I taught sixth grade.

BERNIE: How about that! Where.

CAROL: At the Horace Mann School.

BERNIE: You were at the Horace Mann School?

CAROL: For a year and a half.

BERNIE: And I was right across the street?

CAROL: Where?

BERNIE: At the Garage.
　　The Company Garage is right across the street. I was out there all the time.
　　We used to eat at Mike's. Did you ever go in there?

CAROL: No. I went in for cigarettes once in a while.

BERNIE: I used to go in there all the time. I was there —easily—twice a week.
　　For years.
　　Goddamn.
　　When were you there?

CAROL: 1969.

BERNIE: . . . I haven't worked for the phone company since '55.
　　You want some tea?

CAROL: You have any coffee?

BERNIE: Yeah, sure. Instant.

CAROL: That's fine.

BERNIE: But I bet I saw you around. Boston, Boylston Street . . .

CAROL: We must've seen each other . . . in the Common . . .
　　A hundred times.

## Scene XI

BERNIE: I remember the day you turned twenty-one.
February fourth, 1968.
Your birthday.
I was going to call you up.
You probably don't believe it.
It's not important.
The actions are important.
The present is important.
I spent a couple of days in jail once.
What it taught me, you've gotta be where you are.
. . . While you're there.
Or you're nowhere.
Do you know what I mean?
As it pertains to you and me?
Because I think it's very important. . . .
Does this make any sense to you?

CAROL: I want to get to know you.

BERNIE: And I want to get to know you. But that's not
going to magically wipe out twenty years. . . .
In which you were growing up, which you had to
do anyway, and I was drunk. . . .
I don't mean to get stupid about it.
But let's get up, go out, do this, go look at the

locomotive if they've still got it there, something
. . . you know?
Because, all kidding aside, what's between us isn't
going nowhere, and the rest of it doesn't exist.

## Scene XII

BERNIE: So let me ask you something—you don't mind
if I get personal for a second, do you?

CAROL: What? *(Pause.)*

BERNIE: What I want to know is why all of a sudden
you come looking for me. And it's not that I'm
criticizing you.

CAROL: Why should I think you were criticizing me?

*Pause.*

BERNIE: I mean, I could of come looking for *you* after
you were twenty-one. Not that I was sure how
you'd feel about seeing me . . . but you must of felt
the same way? No.
I mean, it must of been . . . I'm guessing . . . some
kind of decision to get you to all of a sudden come
looking for me.
How did you find me?

CAROL: Through the A.A.

BERNIE: And you just kind of decided and sent Gerry over to meet me?

CAROL: Yes.

BERNIE: And why now?

CAROL: I felt lonely.

BERNIE: . . . Oh. (*Pause.*)

CAROL: You're my father.

# Scene XIII

CAROL: I feel lonely.

*Pause.*

BERNIE: Who doesn't?

CAROL: Do you?

BERNIE: Sometimes.

CAROL: I feel cheated.
And, do you know what? I never had a father.

BERNIE: Carol . . .

CAROL: And I don't want to be pals and buddies; I want you to be my father.

(*Pause.*)
And to hear your goddamn war stories and the whole thing.
And that's why now because that's how I feel.
(*Pause.*)
I'm entitled to it.
Am I?
Am I?

BERNIE: Yes.

CAROL: I am. You're goddamn right.

BERNIE: You know what the important thing is?

CAROL: What?

BERNIE: To be together.
What's past is in the past . . . it's gone.
You're a grown woman . . . I'm on the wagon, your mother's remarried, I got a good job, and there's no reason . . .
I can't make it up to you.

CAROL: Do you have to go to work tonight?

BERNIE: I don't work on Sundays. But Sandy got sick so I was supposed to come in but I called Frank and he told me he'd get someone else to cover so I don't have to go in tonight.
You want to do something?

CAROL: Gerry was . . . he said he'd like it if we went out to dinner.
Would you like that?

BERNIE: Yeah. I'd like that.

CAROL: We could go out by ourselves if you want.

BERNIE: No. It's a good idea I think.
And it's no big thing in any case, right?

CAROL: . . . We could go out, just the two of us.

BERNIE: Whatever you want. What you want, Carol.
That's what we'll do.

## Scene XIV

BERNIE: I got you something. Sit down. I'll give it to
you.

CAROL: What is it?

BERNIE: I don't know. I found it on the bus.

CAROL: . . . It's beautiful.

BERNIE: Yeah.

CAROL (*reading inscription*): "To Carol from her Father. March eighth, 1973."

BERNIE: It's my fault. It's not their fault. My threes look
like eights.
It's only five days off.
It's the thought that counts. . . .
Ruth told me that you should never give anyone
jewelry because then they'll always think they have
to wear it when you're around. . . .
So I never gave her any.

CAROL: It's real gold. . . .
Thank you, Bernie.

BERNIE: I'm not going to tell you you don't have to wear it if you don't like it.
I hope you do like it.

CAROL: I do like it . . .

BERNIE: So what's the weather like out there?

CAROL: It's fine. Just a little chilly.

BERNIE: We should be getting ready, no? Shouldn't you call Gerry?

CAROL: Yes.

BERNIE: So you do that and I'll put away the things and then we'll go.

CAROL: The bracelet's lovely, Bernie.

BERNIE: Thank you.

# DARK PONY

This play is dedicated to Lindsay Crouse

*Dark Pony* opened on October 14, 1977, in a Yale Repertory production, New Haven, Connecticut, with the following cast:

| | |
|---|---|
| THE FATHER | Michael Higgins |
| THE DAUGHTER | Lindsay Crouse |

This production was directed by Walt Jones; set by Kate Edmunds; lighting by William Connor.

### The Characters

THE FATHER
THE DAUGHTER

### The Scene

An automobile.

### The Time

Night.

FATHER: Once upon a time there was an Indian.
  (*Pause.*)
  In the days when wild things roamed the land, and
  long before the White Man came here.

DAUGHTER: When was this?

FATHER: A long, long time ago.
  (*Pause.*)

DAUGHTER (*to self*): Long ago.

FATHER: He was a Brave, and very handsome.

DAUGHTER: What's a Brave?

FATHER: A man who fights in war.
  A young man.
  And his body was like Iron.
  and he could see like an Eagle.
  And he could run like a Deer.
  You ever see a deer run?

DAUGHTER: Sure.

FATHER: And swim like a fish.

DAUGHTER: And he ran like a deer?

FATHER: Yes.

DAUGHTER: Hopping?

FATHER: No. Not hopping. But as fast as deer run when
  they run.

DAUGHTER: And could he hop a fence?

FATHER: He could jump over it. Yes.

DAUGHTER *(to self)*: Good.

FATHER: His name was . . .

FATHER and DAUGHTER *(simultaneously)*: Rain Boy.

FATHER: And he was beloved by all his tribe,
  because he was both brave and gay.
  And he brought happiness to all around him just by
  smiling.
  If the times were bad.
  Or singing songs he used to sing.
  Or telling stories.
  Then he would act out the parts.
  He was a renowned fighter.

DAUGHTER: Who did they fight?

FATHER: Other tribes.

DAUGHTER: The Germans?

FATHER: No.
  And Rain Boy had a special friend.

DAUGHTER: I know.

FATHER: Who?

DAUGHTER: Dark Pony!

FATHER: Yes, Dark Pony.
  When he was in trouble or whenever he found that
  he needed help,

then he would call his friend Dark Pony.
He would say:
"Dark Pony . . ."

FATHER and DAUGHTER (*simultaneously*):    "Dark
Pony, your friend Rain Boy calls to you."

FATHER: Then he'd look up, if they were down
in a valley, or around, if they were in a culvert, or
a stream; or if they were high on a meadow.
He would see a speck. A dark red speck . . .

DAUGHTER (*to self*): Like blood.

FATHER: Red. Like a rose—like sunset in the wheat or
grass.
Galloping towards him.
(*Pause.*)
Dark Pony.
Come to help him.

DAUGHTER (*to self*): "Your friend Rain Boy calls to
you."

FATHER: If he was wounded, pick him up and carry
him away upon his back.
If he was thirsty, bring him cool stream water in a
hide.
If he was hungry, bring him food.

DAUGHTER (*to self*): Something to eat.

FATHER: One day he was bound home after many
moons of fighting in a foreign province.
He had not seen his wife or baby in a long, long
while.

DAUGHTER (*to self*): He missed them.

FATHER: And he longed to see her.
    Up they went.
    Up through the mountains.
    Climbing home.
    Until the snows came.
    Falling early on the homebound Braves—
    It trapped them.

DAUGHTER *(to self)*: In the snow.

FATHER: Up in the mountains.
    Cold.
    Alone.
    Until his enemies all stole away one night;
    They took his food, and told his friends that he had
    died, and crept on through the mountain 'til he was
    alone.
    *(Pause.)*
    In the mountain woods.
    *(Pause.)*
    Starved and weak.
    As he trudged on alone to see his young wife and
    his child.
    Many days.
    Until one night when he had fallen and was set
    upon by wolves.

DAUGHTER: No!

FATHER: He had built a fire so he could rest, and when
    it burnt down he would rise and march again.

DAUGHTER *(to self)*: This was in Winter.

FATHER: When he woke, what did he see? The eyes of
    *wolves*!

DAUGHTER *(to self)*: No.

FATHER: Glaring at him from the darkness.
    Orange eyes and howling.

DAUGHTER: I'm scared.

*Pause.*

FATHER: And they drew closer.
    He cried out with all his strength:
    "Dark Pony, Dark Pony, your friend, Rain Boy,
    calls to you."
    And he looked up.
    But he was alone.
    The wolves came closer.
    He cried:
    "Dark Pony, Dark Pony.
    Your friend, Rain Boy, calls to you."
    The wolves stopped.
    *(Pause.)*
    He lifted up a log from the fire to defend himself,
    but he knew that he couldn't last long.
    He could smell them now.
    *(Pause.)*
    They came closer.
    "Oh," he said.
    *(Pause.)*
    "Oh, Dark Pony . . ."
    *(Pause.)*
    "You have forgotten me."
    Then he heard neighing.
    *(Pause.)*
    Hooves beating through the snow.
    From the highest cliff.

Down through the mountain.
Crying. And galloping.
Borne like the sleet on the wind.
As he fell back exhausted,
The wolves whined.
They tried to flee.

DAUGHTER *(to self)*: They tried to leave.

FATHER: But he bore down upon them.
    *(Pause.)*
    And through their midst.
    *(Pause.)*
    Through the dying fire.
    The snow grew red with their blood.
    *(Pause.)*
    Then all became quiet.
    The wind blew.
    The snow drifted.
    He lay in silence.
    He had become cold.
    Dark Pony walked over to him, and he nudged him
    with his nose.
    *(Pause.)*
    And he neighed.
    *(Pause.)*
    And he licked his face.
    *(Pause.)*
    Slowly he opened his eyes.
    *(Pause.)*
    He looked up above him.
    Dark Pony was standing there.
    *(Pause.)*
    "Oh, Dark Pony," he said . . .
    *(Pause.)*

"I thought you had forgotten me."
(*Pause.*)

DAUGHTER: Are we almost home yet?

FATHER: Yes.
(*Pause.*)
(*To self*) Down from the mountains.
Down.
Across the hills.
Across the prairies.

DAUGHTER: . . . Because I remember how it sounds.

FATHER: You do?

DAUGHTER: The road.

FATHER: Yes.
We are almost there.

DAUGHTER (*to self*): 'Cause I remember how it sounds.

FATHER: . . . Down in the Valleys—he would look above and see his friend there.

DAUGHTER (*to self*): . . . Just before we get home.

*Pause.*

FATHER (*to self*): "Dark Pony,
Rain Boy calls to you."

*Pause.*

DAUGHTER: We are almost home.

# OTHER GROVE PRESS DRAMA AND THEATER PAPERBACKS

B117 BRECHT, BERTOLT / The Good Woman of Setzuan / $1.95 [See also Seven Plays by Bertolt Brecht, GP248 / $12.50]

B80 BRECHT, BERTOLT / The Jewish Wife and Other Short Plays (In Search of Justice, The Informer, The Elephant Calf, The Measures Taken, The Exception and the Rule, Salzburg Dance of Death) / $1.95

B414 BRECHT, BERTOLT / The Mother / $2.95

GP248 BRECHT, BERTOLT / Seven Plays by Bertolt Brecht (In the Swamp, A Man's A Man, Saint Joan of the Stockyards, Mother Courage and Her Children, Galileo, The Good Woman of Setzuan, The Caucasian Chalk Circle) / $12.50

B333 BRECHT, BERTOLT / The Threepenny Opera / $1.95

B193 BULGAKOV, MIKHAIL / Heart of a Dog / $2.95

B147 BULGAKOV, MIKHAIL / The Master and Margarita / $3.95

E693 CHEKHOV, ANTON / The Cherry Orchard / $2.95

E717 CLURMAN, HAROLD, ed. / Seven Plays of the Modern Theater (Waiting for Godot by Samuel Beckett, The Quare Fellow by Brendan Behan, A Taste of Honey by Shelagh Delaney, The Connection by Jack Gelber, The Balcony by Jean Genet, Rhinoceros by Eugene Ionesco, The Birthday Party by Harold Pinter) / $6.95

E159 DELANEY, SHELAGH / A Taste of Honey / $2.95 [See also Seven Plays of the Modern Theater, Harold Clurman, ed., E717 / $6.95]

E380 DURRENMATT, FRIEDRICH / The Physicists / $2.95

E344 DURRENMATT, FRIEDRICH / The Visit / $2.95

B132 GARSON, BARBARA / MacBird! /$1.95

E223 GELBER, JACK / The Connection / $3.95 [See also Seven Plays of the Modern Theater, Harold Clurman, ed., E717 / $6.95]

E130 GENET, JEAN / The Balcony / $2.95 [See also Seven Plays of the Modern Theater, Harold Clurman, ed., E717 / $6.95]

E208 GENET, JEAN / The Blacks: A Clown Show / $2.95 [See also Grove Press Modern Drama, John Lahr, ed., E633 / $5.95]

E577 GENET, JEAN / The Maids and Deathwatch: Two Plays / $3.95

E677 GRIFFITHS, TREVOR / The Comedians / $3.95

B107    MOON, SAMUEL, ed. / One Act: Eleven Short Plays of the Modern Theater (Miss Julie by August Strindberg, Purgatory by William Butler Yeats, The Man With the Flower in His Mouth by Luigi Pirandello, Pullman Car Hiawatha by Thornton Wilder, Hello Out There by William Saroyan, 27 Wagons Full of Cotton by Tennessee Williams, Bedtime Story by Sean O'Casey, Cecile by Jean Anouilh, This Music Crept By Me Upon the Waters by Archibald MacLeish, A Memory of Two Mondays by Arthur Miller, The Chairs by Eugene Ionesco) / $3.95

E605    MROZEK, SLAWOMIR / Striptease, Repeat Performance, and The Prophets / $2.65

E568    MROZEK, SLAWOMIR / Vatzlav / $1.95

E462    NICHOLS, PETER / Joe Egg / $2.95

E650    NICHOLS, PETER / The National Health / $3.95

B400    ORTON, JOE / The Complete Plays (The Ruffian on the Stair, The Good and Faithful Servant, The Erpingham Camp, Funeral Games, Loot, What the Butler Saw, Entertaining Mr. Sloane) / $4.95

E393    ORTON, JOE / Entertaining Mr. Sloane / $2.95 [See also The Complete Plays of Joe Orton, B400 / $4.95]

E470    ORTON, JOE / Loot / $2.95 [See also The Complete Plays of Joe Orton, B400 / $4.95]

E315    PINTER, HAROLD / The Birthday and The Room: Two Plays / $2.95 [See also Seven Plays of the Modern Theater, Harold Clurman, ed., E717 / $6.95]

E299    PINTER, HAROLD / The Caretaker and The Dumb Waiter: Two Plays / $2.95

B402    PINTER, HAROLD / Complete Works: One (The Birthday Party, The Room, The Dumb Waiter, A Slight Ache, A Night Out, The Black and White, The Examination) / $3.95

B403    PINTER, HAROLD / Complete Works: Two (The Caretaker, Night School, The Dwarfs, The Collection, The Lover, Five Revue Sketches) / $3.95

B410    PINTER, HAROLD / Complete Works: Three (Landscape, Silence, The Basement, Six Revue Sketches, Tea Party [play], Tea Party [short story], Mac) / $3.95

E411    PINTER, HAROLD / The Homecoming / $1.95

E555    PINTER, HAROLD / Landscape and Silence: Two Plays / $3.95 [See also Complete Works: Three by Harold Pinter, B410 / $3.95]

E432                                                  Party and The

E663                                    / $1.95
E606                                    / $1.95
E497    SHAW, ROBERT / Man in the Glass Booth / $2.95
E635    SHEPARD, SAM / The Tooth of Crime and Geography
        of a Horse Dreamer: Two Plays / $3.95
E686    STOPPARD, TOM / Albert's Bridge and Other Plays (If
        You're Glad I'll Be Frank, Artist Descending a
        Staircase, Where Are They Now? A Separate Peace) /
        $3.95
E684    STOPPARD, TOM / Dirty Linen and New-Found-Land:
        Two Plays / $2.95
E703    STOPPARD, TOM / Every Good Boy Deserves Favor
        and Professional Foul: Two Plays / $3.95
E489    STOPPARD, TOM / The Real Inspector Hound and
        After Magritte: Two Plays / $3.95
B319    STOPPARD, TOM / Rosencrantz and Guildenstern
        Are Dead / $1.95
E661    STOPPARD, TOM / Travesties / $1.95
B226    TYNAN, KENNETH / Oh! Calcutta! / $1.95
E708    VAN ITALLIE, JEAN-CLAUDE / America Hurrah and
        Other Plays (The Serpent, A Fable, The Hunter and the
        Bird, Almost Like Being) / $5.95
E414    VIAN, BORIS / The Empire Builders / $2.95
E434    VIAN, BORIS / The Generals' Tea Party / $1.95
E62     WALEY, ARTHUR, tr. and ed. / The No Plays of Japan
        / $5.95
E519    WOOD, CHARLES / Dingo / $1.95

## CRITICAL STUDIES

E127    ARTAUD, ANTONIN / The Theater and Its Double /
        $3.95
E441    COHN, RUBY, ed. / Casebook on Waiting for Godot /
        $3.95
E603    HARRISON, PAUL CARTER / The Drama of Nommo:
        Black Theater in the African Continuum / $2.45
E695    HAYMAN, RONALD / How To Read A Play / $2.95
E387    IONESCO, EUGENE / Notes and Counternotes:
        Writings on the Theater / $3.95

GROVE PRESS, INC., 196 West Houston St., New York, N.Y. 10014